Nils Kolkin

Ethereal matter, electricity and akasa

Nils Kolkin

Ethereal matter, electricity and akasa

ISBN/EAN: 9783337733445

Printed in Europe, USA, Canada, Australia, Japan

Cover: Foto ©ninafisch / pixelio.de

More available books at **www.hansebooks.com**

CONTENTS: A NEW DEVICE FOR THE DETECTION OF DIFFERENT CONDITIONS OF ETHEREAL MATTER AND AKASA; APPARENT COMPOSITION OF COSMIC ETHER; SOMETHING NEW ABOUT ELECTRICITY; SOMETHING NEW ABOUT THE HUMAN ORGANISM; LINES OF AKASA OR SUPPOSED ORGANS OF THE SOUL; PSYCHICAL TRANSMISSION OF IDEAS TO A DISTANCE; AND OCCULT TRICKS.

PRICE, 50 CENTS.

FOR SALE BY

THE J. M. PINCKNEY BOOK AND STATIONERY CO.,
414 Fourth Street, Sioux City, Iowa,
AND BY BOOKSELLERS GENERALLY.

Entered according to Act of Congress, in the year 1891, by Nils Kolkin. in the office of the Librarian of Congress, at Washington.

ALL RIGHTS RESERVED.

PREFACE.

The present volume contains popular extracts of "Electricity as a form of Ethereal Matter" by the same author with a treatise on akasa added. The last named work has been widely advertised, but has not yet been published. It must be kept in mind that it is the result of original researches, all undertaken in the Territory of Dakota, and researches of considerable magnitude.

PART I.

MUTUAL INTERCHANGE OF LIGHT, HEAT AND ELECTRICITY ON ONE HAND AND COSMIC ETHER ON THE OTHER.

SECTION I.

NOTIONS OF MATTER.

It is generally believed that there exists a subtle kind of matter which pervades all nature and is found in solids, liquids and gases both in space and in all higher or lower vacua. This form of matter, the existence of which has been inferred from different phenomena, has been called imponderable, as it is believed to have no weight or could not be weighed. It has also been called ether or rather, cosmic ether to distinguish it from a liquid substance of the same name.

It seems as if this ether has, generally, been considered to be a simple and uniform fluid. A somewhat more unreasonable theory has lately been worked out by Sir William Thompson and others, who consider it to be an elastic solid which fills the whole universe, and who try to illustrate all physical phenomena by the vibrations of an elastic solid. It may be remarked that this theory was held to be orthodox in Sir William Thompson's time.

In physical research, the guiding theory is of great importance. Many forces in nature have not been utilized, or have become only partially known on account of incorrect theories. A correct view of that which is not yet perfectly known can most safely be obtained by conclusions drawn from that which is well known. What is our notion of matter? We think of matter as something that occupies space and, where it occupies space, excludes everything else which may be called matter. If cosmic ether be matter, it can not exist in the same space that is occupied by an atom of coarser matter. If ether be found in the interior of a solid, it can be found only in the interstices between the atoms or molecules. When we look at the visible nature, we do not find that matter is uniform. It has from the very beginning appeared to us as multiform. With what right can we throw away any of our knowledge of matter, when we are to form a theory of a division of the same, that has only been thought to exist, but has not been known? Visible matter consists of elements and compounds of them, and this can be said of that which is partly visible, as the gases. Why should not this be true of cosmic ether? Analogous theories must be used for that which is analogous, is the rule. We can formulate the theory blindfolded, that ethereal matter consists of elements and compounds thereof, as surely as it can be called matter. The burden of proof does not rest on one who follows this law of analogy.

The field of the unknown was boldly entered on by Sir Isaac Newton, a man ahead of his time. He succeeded in seperating white light into its different component elements by letting it pass through a wedge of glass, or what is now generally called a prism. His theory was that light was matter, and that the different colors, into which light dissolved itself, were different kinds of matter. This theory was too much for his time and was not accepted. Indisputable proofs were needed to give confidence in his theories at that time. Such proofs presented themselves in the case of his theory of gravitation; but his theory of light had to yield place to some more unnatural ones, studied out by book-learned men that lacked his scrutinizing observation and reasoning power.

We are now able to prove the correctness of Newton's theory, and, as this answers many questions in regard to the production of electricity, we shall give a systematic exposition of the relation which exists between light, heat, electricity, and other phenomena of ethereal matter.

Ethereal matter appears to serve as the binding material or cement, so to speak, which holds the minute parts of coarser matter together, so that they form gaseous, liquid, or solid bodies. In this case, it exists in the form of ethereal compounds, consisting of different elements which are, more or less, liberated by the decomposition of the coarser substance. The ethereal elements are nothing but the different elements that produce light and heat. Electricity, of which there are two kinds, is considered a fluid even by orthodox physicists, and these two kinds are different compounds of certain ethereal elements. While electricity resembles a fluid, other ethereal compounds form more coherent masses, as is indicated by astatic pendulums, and can not be called fluids.

Akasa appears as a coarser state of matter than electricity. It is not known to have been detected except in connection with animal bodies, though it exists, without doubt, as an invisible part of a vegetable. It is also believed that akasa is the soul that governs the different growths and formations in the so-called "inorganic" world, as the formations of crystals.

SECTION II.

MEANS OF DETECTING FEEBLE FORCES IN NATURE.

While some physicists hold that ethereal matter is an imponderable fluid, pervading all nature, others seem to be of the opinion that it is only a rarified gas; at least, they speak in that way. Whatever theory be correct, we can show that there are currents of some kind of matter in the atmosphere, when the air does not partake of the same motion, which last may be shown by clouds of smoke. That these manifestations are currents, we know, because they, in all respects, behave like currents. There can not be a current without some kind of matter that flows. To say that we can not be sure that there is anything, as long as we see nothing, which has often been said about electricity, is untenable. There are certain safe rules for drawing conclusions within certain limits, which only the ignorant will think of disputing. To explain these rules belongs to a practical treatise on logic. We may state that this supposed matter can not be detected, except when it is in motion.

This matter, which may have a motion independent of that of the air which it pervades, is what has been called ethereal matter in this work. This matter we naturally suppose to be lighter than the air in which we experiment and, on account of its lightness, we can not expect to observe its motions as easily as we would motions of air. A current of air could be shown by the deflection of a light body, as a feather or a streamer; but any deflection of the lightest body could not be expected to be effected by motions of ethereal matter, before the inertia of the body were overcome.

We will call the attention of the reader to the fact, that

it is customary in physical experiments, when the effect of very slight forces on very light bodies is to be shown, to overcome the inertia of those bodies. An electric current, passing over a wire, has a magnetic action, but a very slight one. To show it, a hole is bored through a glass plate and up through this the conductor is drawn, while iron filings are spread over the plate. An electric current through the wire will have a magnetic action on the iron filings; but the force will be too feeble to start them, before their inertia is overcome by thumping the glass plate with the fingers, when the iron filings will move toward the wire. Another example may be given. If a plumb line be suspended over a sluggish current of water, so that the plumb dips into it, it will be found that the current can not move the plumb line, before its inertia is overcome by vibration of its support. It will then oscillate back and forth in the direction of the current.

Is it possible, by overcoming the inertia of a light pendulum consisting of a fiber with a suitable weight, to observe currents of invisible matter that pervades the air and is yet, to some extent, independent of it? It must be done in this way, if in any. There are many difficulties in the way; but it can be done. The reasons why it has not been noticed more generally are probably two: a general belief in some mystic attraction or repulsion, where the motions of light bodies can not be explained in an ordinary way, and the fact that the existence of a current can be ascertained only by observations at different points. We may here remind the reader of frequent discussions touching the cause of the peculiar motions of pendulums held by the hand. The inertia of a pendulum will be overcome by the trembling of the hand; but as in this case, there may be a greater, though inconscious, movement of the hand in one direction, the oscillation of the pendulum can not be depended on. However, it has been shown that a person may be so unbiased that no inconscious muscular action takes place, except a uniform trembling of the hand, which consists of motions in all possible directions. The oscillation of the pendulum is then determined by forces outside of the hand, either by motions of air or by currents of invisible matter pervading the air If the air be in motion, dust or a cloud of smoke will show this. The method of testing the reliability of such experiments consists in producing currents or vortices of supposed ethereal matter without the knowledge of the experimenter and letting him detect them. A more reliable way of overcoming the inertia of the pendulum is, however, desirable. We shall mention several more or less perfect means of doing this.

Before we go further, we must mention that the atmosphere may be in two different conditions; one in which motions of ethereal matter may be detected with more or less ease, and another in which they can not be detected, and a pendulum, suspended from a vibrating support tends to hang still. The atmosphere is more frequently in such a condition that motions of ethereal matter can not be detected, than otherwise. This is another reason why we, for many years to come, must expect to hear the detection of motions of ethereal matter spoken of as humbug; for, very perfect instruments for registration are not likely to be made soon, as there are no pecuniary inducements.

A pendulum, suspended from a generally vibrating support, has a tendency to hang still, when the atmosphere is cloudy, moist and cold, or sultry in the summer time. This is also the case in the dark and also in deep shadows. A current may be detected where it enters and leaves a shadow, but not in the shadow itself, when it is deep. If such unfavorable conditions of the atmosphere are not very serious, they can be neutralized by heat, light, strong odors, or the friction of certain substances; but, in extreme cases, neutralization is effected only by a large flame or fire. When the barometer is low, the atmosphere is unfavorable. As it rises, favorable moments occur at regular intervals, and these favorable periods become longer, as it continues to rise, until the unfavorable periods have dwindled down to nothing.

Akasa also prevents the detection of currents of ethereal matter, as it is coarser and has more effect on a pendulum. Akasa may be freed from its connection with the body by stroking something; but it is more apt to prevent experiments when it emanates directly from the body, which happens during excitement or curiosity. It has either a movement of its own, which may be detected in the most unfavorable atmosphere, or it prevents the detection of any currents. On account of the mischief done by movements of akasa, it is impossible to undertake experiments in the presence of people, except they are devoid of curiosity and entirely self contained. A mechanical pendulum instrument will be just as much affected as the most unscientific device.

When the atmosphere is favorable, a pendulum, consisting of a fiber or string with a suitable weight or knob of any material or shape, as a watch key or a plumb, will indicate movements of what we have called ethereal akasa or matter, if the inertia of the knob be properly overcome by vibration of its support. Inertia has two components, a horizontal and a vertical one. Both these should be overcome or neutralized, and care should be taken that no greater impetus be given to the pendulum in one direction than in others. This is, of course, best effected by accurate mechanism. When the inertia of a pendulum is properly overcome, it may be said to be astaticized or rendered astatic.

As those who wish to undertake experiments will find so many difficulties in their way that they are apt to give it up in disgust, we will mention several methods of rendering pendulums partially astatic. It will be noticed that such bodies as wooden balls or birds, suspended by elastic strings inside of glass cases, have some peculiar motions. Such pendulums are partially astatic and have the same general motion as more perfectly astaticized pendulums. Small pendulums suspended from larger ones, as from chandeliers, are partially astaticized. If the smaller pendulum contains an elastic string, the vertical component of inertia is also overcome. Glass penduncles that are found on some chandeliers behave in a peculiar manner. They hang still, except a few, and they all swing by turn.

What we have called motions of ethereal matter seems to be nothing else than what is, generally, called electric currents. During storms there are such currents in the direction of the storm; but a wire, laid in that direction, collects a stronger current around the wire than in the air generally, which is also the case with ethereal motions or currents, artificially produced in the air. Such general currents through the atmosphere nearly always commence and end respectively before the storm does, and make experiments on artificial or smaller currents impossible.

If we place two plates, respectively of zinc and copper and both moistened with sulphuric or other acid, a distance apart so that they face each other, there will be an electric current, through the air, from the zinc to the copper and an astatic pendulum will oscillate in that direction, when placed in the current, if the atmosphere be favorable. If the distance between the plates is great enough, a deep shadow may be produced half way between them, and there it will be found that no current is indicated.

When an electric current is sent over a wire, it swells to a certain distance outside of the wire. This may also be observed by means of an astatic pendulum; but it must be so short that it is nearly entirely within the current. In fact, these pendulums should always be short. Electric charges, though they be very slight, may also be detected by the same means, as they always swell into the air and rotate around an axis which is paralell to that of the earth, for which reason an astatic pendulum will circulate around when over the center of the charge. This, however, depends on the latitude of the place where the experiments are made.

To find toward what direction the current flows, is not always possible by the method described, though a pendulum is thrown a trifle farther in that direction. We must, here, describe another way of detecting electric currents in the air. This is by means of pendulums, suspended from a steady support, care being taken that they hang from a smooth surface or that there are no obstacles on any side. When they are put in oscillation, the direction of the oscillation changes gradually, until it coincides with that of the current. But the atmosphere must be favorable, or else it keeps its original direction. This swinging pendulum should also be short.

All currents are stronger at the center than at the sides or at the periphery. If a fixed pendulum be suspended in one side of an electric current, which is entirely in the air or is swelling outside of a conductor, and then put in oscillation at right angles with the current, the stronger force of the current at the center will push the pendulum steadily in one direction, which produces a gradual change in the oscillation. The way the pendulum turns indicates toward what point the current flows.

The atmosphere is favorable for experiments, when the barometer is high, the sky clear, and weather calm and warm or mild, but, even then, experiments often fail on the shaded side of a building. As a rule, the atmosphere is favorable, when the full moon is in or near the meridian and there is an appearance of aurora borealis in the sky. That which makes the atmosphere unfavorable has been called ethereal clouds and is supposed to be some compounds of ethereal matter that have not the nature of a fluid.

PART II.

THE ELEMENTS FORMING THE BASIS OF ELECTRICITY.

SECTION I.

EXPERIMENTS ON LIGHT AND OBSCURE RADIATIONS.

The first one, in the history of science, who conceived the idea of separating sunlight into its component elements by letting it pass through a wedge of glass, was Sir Isaac Newton. He, evidently, got the idea because he thought light was matter. After white or clear light has passed through this wedge, the elements are found separated and are projected on any surface behind the wedge. This visible arrangement of the elements is called the spectrum. In this, heat is detected in the direction of the original ray of light; but, as the different rays of light are separated in passing through the wedge, some being crowded more or less toward the thin edge of the wedge, the common signs of the different elements, except three, appear in the following order: heat, red light, yellow light, blue light, and violet light. The three elements next to the thin edge of the wedge have no visible signs, but the next last seems to produce coolness. The heat and the colors are not due to the elements themselves, but rather to compounds which they have formed and which produce certain impressions; the elements themselves are invisible. Adjacent colors overlap each other, and thus the colors orange and green are produced. Violet is also a mixed color; but we have to put this down as the sign of the place of one certain element in the spectrum. It is produced by a production of red at that place, which is overlapped by the adjacent blue. At the same time that this spectrum is produced, there is a narrower one which is crowded the other way from the thick end of the wedge. This we may call a secondary spectrum.

Instead of a wedge we may use a three-sided bar of glass which is called a prism. Here, the secondary spectrum is of most importance, as it is very bright on account of its being crowded and narrow. The natural spectrum is visible or not according to the angle at which the light enters the prism. A bright and narrow spectrum is best, where it is to be studied by sight; but, for our experiments, a more diffused one is needed.

If we let a broad spectrum fall on a surface, we find that the element, indicated by the heat band, makes the surface electropositive, and there are currents directly in to it from the air which come from a certain distance. These currents vary in length according to the atmosphere; but they always have a certain proportion to the length of the currents that run to or from the other parts of the spectrum. We may represent the length of the currents, drawn by the element indicated by the heat band, by 2—about 2 decimeters; then we have proportional figures for the length of the other currents.

The element, indicated by red light, makes a surface electronegative, and this band sends out currents that have the length of 5 proportional units. The element, indicated by yellow, draws currents of the length of 1 unit; the blue band draws currents of the length of 6 units. The element, indicated by violet, sends out currents of the length of 7 units; the next element, without any visible sign, sends out currents of the length of 5 units. The element next to the last draws currents of the length of 12 units, and the last sends out currents of the length of 4 units.

We have no names for these elements, except those of their indicators in the spectrum. We use those names as far as they go; but we have named the sixth and seventh elements respectively *actin* and *solidin*. The sixth may, probably, be incorrectly named; but the seventh is indicated by a slight cold and appears in connection with the dissolution of very hard substances in a greater quantity than in other cases.

At both ends of the spectrum, are also currents from and to the surface on which the spectrum is projected. These currents are eddy currents, which are always found around currents of ethereal matter, and extend infinitely. On any side of the spectrum, they have the same length and the same width as that of the adjacent band in the spectrum, and each successive space of the width of that band has currents in opposite directions.

Between adjacent elements in the spectrum, there is a point without currents, if the two elements have opposite electric effects, as the red and the yellow. The currents in both bands become gradually shorter toward a point somewhere near the middle of the orange. Between the yellow and the blue which have similar electric effects, there is no point without currents; but those of the blue band become gradually shorter, until they reach the length of the yellow band. In this and similar cases; it is difficult to say where the dividing line between the adjacent elements really is.

These 8 elements which we find in the spectrum may be projected in the same order without the refraction of a visible ray of light or the production of a visible spectrum. Anything placed behind a prism or wedge will have an obscure radiation strong enough to produce an "invisible spectrum" on a surface in front of the prism. This may be studied by means of an astatic pendulum or also a fixed pendulum.

A ray or a pencil of light, passing into a dark room, is in every respect a current, or it produces a current. This may be observed in the same way as electric currents in the air. We may also mention, that there are such currents in the direction of the rays of the sun at daybreak. There is often a noticeable movement of air in the same direction at that time; but the currents of electricity or ethereal matter seem to be due to the rays, and not to the movement of air.

We notice also that what we have called ethereal compounds, odors, electric charges, and even electric currents have obscure radiations that will produce an "invisible spectrum." Again, we find that light and obscure radiations are convertible into electricity and will break up or strengthen what we have called ethereal clouds. A ray of light, sufficiently condensed, is an electric current. Electric currents, both voltaic, dynamic, and atmospheric, are nothing but movements of ethereal matter of no definite composition. Some forms of ethereal matter need some coarser matter to lean on, as they are easily broken up into simple elements and dispersed; thus we find rarified air a poorer conductor of electricity than copper or iron. Some substances are poor conductors, however, in spite of their compactness, as glass. As a rule the hardest and the loosest substances are not good conductors.

The visible white light can not be said to be due to a mixture of pure ethereal elements; the pure elements are invisible. The colors are evidently caused by compounds of simple elements, and white and black must also be put down as colors. Black reflects obscure radiations as much as white; and blue, as much as yellow, in spite of the greater darkness of blue.

The invisible elements in obscure radiations and rays of light become partly separated, when the rays fall obliquely on a surface and are reflected. If they are projected on a second surface, they produce nearly as plain currents as in an ordinary "invisible spectrum;" but the "invisible spectrum" may be several yards long.

We will not attempt to explain why the different invisible elements separate on passing through a prism; but the separation by deflection is illustrated when we throw sand obliquely against a surface. Here, the coarser and finer sand separates and gathers to different sides, as it falls to the ground.

SECTION II.

CLASSES OF ETHEREAL COMPOUNDS.

If we give a piece of red paper a lead pencil polish, we will see a blue color in the polish, when we look at the surface at a certain angle against the light. If a blue paper is treated in the same way, a red or chocolate color appears in the polish, when seen against the daylight. Here, there seems to be a production of a color on account of the repulsion of certain elements by another below the surface. It shows also that a substance, for some reason, can crowd back certain rays of light, while others are allowed to pass or are used in the structure itself.

A surface color, that appears only when seen at a certain angle with the surface, indicates a repulsion of that particular element for one reason or other. About the natural color of a substance, which is not only on its surface, we can say very little. Color, like odor, seems to do no service in keeping the molecules or the atoms of a substance together. It seems to be only an ornament, and Mother Nature says very little about it.

Ethereal compounds may be divided into two classes: those that are only connected with certain coarser matter and those that are free. The first class are those that serve as the binding material of the atoms and molecules of coarser matter or exist only as an ornament around certain substances from which they can not be separated without destruction. The second class are those that can exist in connection with different substances with which they only seem to have a temporary relation, and may, or may not, change the appearance of the substance with which they are connected. Of the free ethereal compounds, there are two kinds: those that change the appearance of tnat with which they are connected, and those that never do so. To the former kind belong the troublesome ethereal clouds that often prevent experiments that we have before described. It is some of them that change liquids to solids, and contract solid bodies in proportion to this amount in the air. To the latter kind belong positive and negative electricity and others.

The ethereal compounds that are not free, as we have called it, are formed in the structure of the coarser matter where they belong, or on the surface. They may be separated or liberated by friction and corrosion, when they may exist as compounds for a longer or shorter time. They form ethereal clouds that are easily detected, but keep sinking downward slowly, as they are affected by gravitation. As it might be believed that these clouds are only molecules of coarser matter, we may state that they sink through material that is impervious to the lightest gases. They are also decomposed and dispersed when ethereal compounds of an opposite character is brought in among them.

The invisible elements may be separated into two divisions: those that produce positive electricity and those that produce negative. When decomposed, the ethereal compounds that contain more of the first kind also produce more positive electricity, and the opposite is true of those that contain more of the last kind. The composition with reference to these two different classes of elements determines, to a great extent, the ability of one compound to neutralize another, as opposite kinds are destructive of each other. There is no compound, however, so generally destructive as that which is connected with heat.

As ethereal compounds are constantly changing in a certain systematic way, when they are not decomposed, we can produce an "invisible spectrum" of them by holding a paper into an ethereal cloud and then placing it behind a prism, or by rubbing two pieces of the same material over a place behind the prism. The proportion of the elements are shown by the width of each band, where they are projected.

Whether we shall put down akasa as an ethereal compound or a product of another class, we can not say. There are so many curious phenomena connected with akasa that its physical composition has not been looked after. Its composition is more fixed than that of ethereal compounds that have been examined.

SECTION III.

THE TWO KINDS OF ELECTRICITY.

An electric current is only a flow of a mixture of various kinds of ethereal matter and has no definite composition. It has been shown that currents from different batteries are so different that they produce very different effects, quantity and force being the same.

The word electricity was first applied to static electricity, to charges of positive or negative electricity, produced by friction, or to sparks produced by the same. The original word, according to some, seems to have been *alak te re*, soul of matter.*

*Anatol Trolladeen and others.

As the friction of amber was often used to produce *alak*, literally soul-gush, the Greek seem to have called that substance *elektron*.

Positive and negative electricity are two common conditions, into which all forms of ethereal matter are thrown more or less during the process of changing.

The invisible ethereal elements we may designate by numbers corresponding to their places in the spectrum, commencing from the heat band, where we have No. 1. Nos. 1, 3, 4, and 7 produce positive electricity, and a spectrum, produced by a positive charge, gives only these elements with nothing but a trace of the others. Nos. 2, 5, 6, and 8 produce negative electricity and are found in its spectrum.

The elements of one of these classes are seldom found free from a mixture of the others. For this reason we can never produce one kind of electricity without producing some of the other.. The elements that have the greater quantity produce their kind of electricity around the most convenient point or material basis that can serve to hold the charge. The other class produce their electricity in the air around the main charge and also on points of coarser matter, if there be any in that place. In taking a spectrum of the central charge it makes some difference, whether the wedge or prism is brought within the surrounding air charge, or is outside of it.

The two kinds of electricity have a mutual tendency to neutralize each other; but still they are mutually attracted. If we produce a certain amount of the two kinds of electricity by the friction of two substances, as silk and glass, and impart some of it respectively to two pit balls that are suspended near each other by silk fibers, as silk is a poor conductor, the pit balls are seen to attract each other, which is plainly caused by the different charges imparted to them. The same attraction is also noticed, if we let a wire simultaneously touch two balls or other two objects, thus charged. However, we find this peculiarity that the negative electricity runs through the wire to the positive; but never the positive, to the negative. This may be observed by means of an astatic pendulum, as the current swells outside of the wire and is discharged from the end near the positive charge. It helps us to understand this phenomenon better, when we consider positive electricity as a fluid of a more viscous character than the other. Practically, positive electricity never runs toward the negative, though it may have a tendency to approach it. This can never be observed, as negative electricity never leaves time for it.

The construction of an electric battery is easily understood from these two different peculiarities of negative and positive electricity. If we put a copper plate in dilute sulphuric acid, the ethereal matter, set free by the corrosion of the copper, produces a charge of positive electricity in the vessel. If we put a zinc plate in dilute sulphuric acid in another vessel or jar, this produces negative electricity. We have then two electrostatic batteries. We may connect these jars or vessels by means of a wire and use the two as one ordinary battery; but it is customary to have the two different plates in the same jar.

The negative electricity, that is produced around the zinc plates, runs all the time over to the positive plate through the acid. As electricity is a fluid, consequently matter, it must seek an outlet, and it is found to be discharged into the air from the top of the copper plate. The current here discharged is already a mixture of ethereal matter; for the positive and negative electricity has already been broken up by the union. Air is not a very good conductor of electricity, and we may fasten a wire to the top of the copper plate. The current will then flow out through this and be discharged at the end. This may be observed with an astatic pendulum. An electric current is very sluggish, so to speak, with nothing but this short wire as a path. It is discharged into the air all the way from the battery. If we can lengthen the wire so that we can dip the extreme end of it into a tank or pond, we find that the current begins to run with greater force and swells less outside of the wire, because it has plenty of matter of good conductively to escape over. The rapidity of the current, that starts from the negative plate, naturally, produces a suction of ethereal matter down through that plate. This may also be observed by means of an astatic pendulum. We can increase the force and volumn of the current considerably by fastening a wire of the length of a yard to the negative plate; but, if it is very long, there is need of too much force to draw the ethereal matter that, naturally, comes over the wire.

In practice, however, the wire from the positive plate is bent around, so that the other end is fixed to the negative plate. The current then runs through the battery again. This arrangement is called the electric circuit.

We easily see that the attraction of the positive electricity on the negative in the battery serves as the motive power. As the positive electricity draws a current from the negative, and the negative moves and gives the current, its moving force, the names *tractin* and *motin* have been proposed instead of the unwieldy names we have.

These substances that are good conductors of electricity are also suitable substances for holding electric charges. Some substances, as glass, gutta-percha, silk, dry air, and dry paper and wood, are very poor conductors and are used to insulate the conductors for electricity from substances of good conductivity, whereby the current or charge is prevented from escaping. Metals, as a rule, are good conductors.

SECTION IV.

THE PRODUCTION OF ELECTRICITY.

The proportion of ethereal elements in positive electricity seems to be: 12 parts of No. 7; 6 of No. 4; 2 of No. 1; and 1 of No. 3. The proportion of elements in negative electricity seems to be: 7 of No. 5; 5 of No. 2; 5 of No. 6; and 4 of No. 8. Of course, it is difficult to get exact figures, as we do not know the exact dividing line between the elements in the spectrum.

Sunlight will sometimes produce more positive, and sometimes more negative electricity, according to the changes in the radiation and the state of the medium in which the electricity is produced. The pure elements do not produce electricity or any other ethereal combination, except they are brought to a state of rest. This is, to some extent, true of visible light; but a dense atmosphere is enough to arrest light somewhat, while obscure radiations pass through even opaque bodies. Positive electricity has its greatest strength in the less refrangible part of the spectrum, while the negative has its strength in the other part.

It is on surfaces, especially of opaque bodies, that electricity is formed. This is not due to the arrest of light, however, so much as to the repulsion of certain ethereal elements by different substances. On the surface of every body, or around it, as a charge swells outside of the body that holds it, there is a slight charge of electricity which is natural to the substance. This surface electricity with its surrounding opposite electricity is different from that produced by the decomposition of the substance. If the electricity produced by decomposition be more positive, the surface electricity is more negative, and *vice versa*.

On account of the surface electricity, we can make dry batteries by connecting two different pieces of metal; but the current produced in this way is weaker than when the metals are acted on by acid. Here, the current also has an opposite direction; it is from the copper to the zinc, as the surface of copper is negative, and that of zinc positive.

Colors modify the natural surface electricity. Here, blue is positive, and red negative. Those substances that are easily dissolved also have a modified surface electricity.

Heat, when applied to metals and water, produces positive electricity; but this does not seem to be due to the heat itself, but to its action on the ethereal binding material in those substances. Heat attacks what we have called *solidin* which is an important element of positive electricity.

If we place one cup of cold water, and one of warm, beside each other and connect them by means of a wire, there is a current from the cold to the warm cup; but if we put a piece of ice in the cold cup, this becomes more positive. This is due to the dissolution of the ice. The same takes place if we put salt or sugar into the cold cup. The positive effect of heat seems to be due to its neutralization of those ethereal compounds that produce solidification. Hot air in the summer time is often negative or sultry, as it is called, but the heating of cold air produces positive electricity.

The natural electricity, produced on the surface of the following metals, is positive, becoming more negative toward the end of the list: sodium, magnesium, zinc, lead and tin. When they are decomposed, they produce negative electricity in the same order. The following substances have a negative surface, becoming more positive toward the end of the list: glass, carbon, platinum, gold, silver copper, and iron. When decomposed, they produce positive electricity in the same order.

When two substances of about the same electric character are placed in juxtaposition with each other, their electric difference becomes greater. We can produce a current with carbon and platinum, though both are positive in acid; but platinum would be more negative than carbon.

Friction has not been used to produce currents, but charges. Two pieces of the same substance may be rubbed together; but the electric effect is greater, if a positive and a negative substance be rubbed together, on account of the effect of juxtaposition. If we rub the following substances, the first in the list is the most positive; and the last, the least: cat's skin, wool, ivory, glass, cotton, silk, wood, the different metals, caoutchouc, sealing wax, resin, and leather.

SECTION V.

THE RENEWAL OF ETHEREAL BINDING MATERIAL IN THE STRUCTURE OF MATTER.

Ethereal compounds undergo a steady change in a certain order. This takes place in free ethereal compounds and in the structure of coarse matter. They may change from one place to another in a certain system; but they are also broken up and replaced by new ones of the same kind in a certain order, while the discarded elements and compounds are thrown out to considerable distances.

We can plainly show that an electric charge is renewed. If we charge a ball with positive electricity, we find that negative electricity is formed around it, which constantly sends currents into the charge. This would have the effect of neutralizing the charge; but it is not found to decrease for a very long time, if the insulation is good. If we impart only a small charge to a piece of iron and enclose it in a glass bottle, where the discarded compounds can not be entirely thrown out, we will find, after a day or more, that the charge has increased.

The renewal of ethereal binding material in some substances is more rapid than in others. Some substances throw out exhausted ethereal matter farther than others. In the following list steel has the greatest effect in throwing "refuse ethereals": steel, stone, bone, iron, and copper. If we fix two tin plates at different ends of a wire, we can produce a current through the wire in any direction by standing at a distance and turn the flat side of a steel plate toward any of the tin plates. This current ceases, when we turn the edge toward them. Lead has a greater effect than steel in this experiment; but it produces an opposite electric effect to that when it is decomposed, which the substances in the preceding list do not.

All this renewal may seem to be a freak of nature, but it

is, no doubt, a necessity. It requires power or energy to hold the molecules tightly together. Energy, however, can not be used eternally without being renewed.

When electricity is produced by the friction of glass and the action of acid on carbon, this is due more to the disturbance of the renewing material than to the decomposition of those substances.

PART III.

THE LAWS OF ELECTRICITY.

SECTION I.

ELECTRIC CHARGES.

Electric charges are said to be static or standing still. It will be seen that this is not literally true.

If we impart a positive charge to a moist paper ball, suspended by a silk fiber, we find that it forms a sphere around the ball. This sphere rotates around an axis, parallel to that of the earth. This may be observed by means of an astatic pendulum. The diameter of this sphere may be from an inch to some yards. All around the central sphere is a region of opposite electricity, which has a depth equal to the diameter of the central sphere. This negative region, supposing the center to be positive, consists of nothing but currents that run inward to the periphery of the positive sphere. The central sphere with the surrounding covering of opposite electricity forms a perfect sphere, which we may call an *electrosphere* The diameter of an electrosphere is always 3 times that of the central sphere. All flames, as a candle or lamp light, have always positive electrospheres.

If we impart a negative charge to the ball or suspend a small piece of zinc that is moistened with acid, we find a central sphere of outwardly running currents. This sphere of currents is surrounded by a layer of more positive electricity. The layer has a depth equal to the diameter of the central sphere of currents. This is a negative electrosphere.

By examination of the surroundings we find that an electrosphere has a position in the center of a rotating cylinder of ethereal matter. This cylinder has an infinite axial extension and a diameter 3 times that of the electrosphere.

The rotation of the cylinder with the electrosphere is produced by an east going current of ethereal matter around the earth. It, therefore, moves eastward with the lower side, and westward with the upper.

If we charge a cylindrical body or a long rod, there is no electrosphere produced. It will have a cylindrical charge with currents in the center or outside, according to the nature of the charge, and the charge will produce similar currents in axial directions infinitely. The cylinder revolves, if it be brought somewhat parallel to the axis of the earth. Then the rotating cylinder will also have a diameter 3 times that of the double cylindrical charge and 9 times that of the central charge.

SECTION II.

CURRENTS IN CONDUCTORS.

If we charge two bodies differently and then connect them by wire, we find a current over the wire which swells outside of it. As soon as the current ceases, we give the two bodies a greater charge, and the diameter of the current is increased.

If we connect a plate of copper and a plate of zinc we have a constant current over the wire. If we substitute an iron plate for the one of copper, but of the same size, the current gets a greater diameter. This is not due to a greater production of electricity, in this case, but to the fact that the current runs with less force; for the surface of iron is nearly as positive as that of zinc and there is too little attraction. The amount of electricity in both was the same, we will say; for the amount of fluid passing in a current is measured by the sectional area multiplied by the velocity.

If the force of an electric current be the same, we can find the relative amount of electricity from the sectional area of the currents.

The diameter of a current also varies as the conductivity of the conductor used. If we use a fine wire, the current swells. If we substitute one of iron for one of copper, the diameter of the current is also increased, because iron has less conductivity than copper. To find the relative quantity of electricity that passes in a current, we must know the force of the battery, the resistance of the circuit or the conductor, and the sectional area of the current.

Loss of current is caused by very sharp turns in the conductor and also by gradual ramification of the conductor which terminate in the air or are connected with the ground.

In the practical application of electricity, the resistance of the circuit is of great importance. It is found by comparison with a known resistance. It is plain that, if the current be given two paths, and half of it goes over one and half of it over the other, the resistances of those two paths must be like.

Resistance tends to waste a current by forcing it into the air; velocity or electromotive force tends to send it through the resistance, thereby saving it. The rule is that the current, after passing over a circuit, will have a strength equal to the electromotive force, divided by the resistance. For the measurement of electromotive force, resistance and quantity, there are numerous instruments, and certain units have been agreed upon.

The unit of quantity is called *ampere;* that of electromotive force, *volt;* and that of resistance, *ohm.* If we wish to send a current to a station 5 miles off through a wire that has a resistance of 48 ohms, and we have a battery whose electromotive force is 1 volt and has also a resistance of 2 ohms, making the total resistance 50 ohms, the current at the other station will be 1 divided by 50, equal to 1-50 ampere.

If the telegraph apparatus, there, could not be worked with less than 1-20 ampere, we would have to make use of more batteries and let the current from one run through the other. If we put them side by side and produce a ramification of the conductor by using a wire for each battery and fastening them to the main line, we would only swell the current, and there would be nothing more than 1-50 ampere at the other station. If one of the batteries had more electromotive force than one volt, there might be a little stronger current at the other end. If the current runs from one battery through the next &c., the electromotive force of all is added together.

SECTION III.

VARIOUS CLASSES OF CURRENTS.

A well made classification, and corresponding nomenclature, is not only valuable, but absolutely necessary, in order to explain and discuss phenomena without embarrassment.

Primary and secondary currents.—The currents produced directly by a generator of electricity, whether through the air or a special conductor are *primary*. An electric current always tends to have a cylindrical form, and this is always the case, when the conductor is a wire. Outside of the primary current, however, is a movement of ethereal matter in the opposite direction like an eddy. The ethereal matter that moves that way forms a cylindrical layer around it like a tubing that is drawn in the opposite direction to that of the primary current. The thickness of this tubing is equal to one half of the diameter of the primary current. If a wire be stretched in this tubular eddy, it will take up considerable of it and will keep a current, even where it is outside of the eddy. Such a current is called a *secondary current*. The current is also said to be "induced."

The tubular eddy has another eddy outside of it that runs in the same direction as the primary current. These eddies and counter-eddies keep on infinitely. If the primary current be suddenly shut off, the nearest eddies sink together and occupy the wire by turn, when there are currents back and forth for some time.

If we take a large metal bar and give the ends different surface electrification, there will be a weak current from one end to the other. This current we may suppose to be entirely in the bar; but, by examination, we find that there is current in the same direction outside of it a distance from the surface which is equal to the diameter of the bar. We might think that it would be right to call this the "swell" of the current; but it is not.

If we prolong the path of the current by fixing a fine wire to the center of the most positive end of the bar, the current proceeds over this wire. Here, it has a "swell," because the diameter of the current is more than three times that of the wire. If the whole primary current has only a diameter 3 times that of the conductor, the outside current consists only of ethereal matter carried along by the *current proper*. The outside flow, in this case, we may call a *carried current*.

When a conductor is used that has so much conductivity that there is no swell to a given current, but only a *carried* flow outside, which gives the whole primary current a diameter only 3 times that of the conductor, we may say that we use an *adequate conductor*. If there is a swell in the current, the conductor is *inadequate*. For practical purposes, we must not take the word "inadequate" to mean that the conductor can not be used.

If we keep a current passing through a steel bar or any other hard substance for a certain time, it will have a similar current through it, after the battery current is shut down, and will keep it for a great length of time. This current is, evidently, due to the direction in which exhausted ethereal matter is thrown, after it has been acted on by an electric current. This we call a *fixed current*. A permanent magnet has a fixed current around it.

Various conditions of currents.—In a circuit, the current in a battery is called the *internal* current; and that outside, the *external*. That part of the whole conductor or path in a circuit which is occupied by the battery, is called the internal conductor; and the whole circuit outside of the battery, the *external circuit*.

For the sake of discussing phenomena in nature, we may use this classification. When we have a positive plate at one end of a wire, and a negative at the other, while the current is between them, we may call this an *inter-elementary* current. Whatever flows past the positive generator may be called a trans-elementary current or an extension of the current. As there is flow of ethereal matter to the negative plate or generator from the air, this may be called a *drawn* current.

If a current be varied in any way so as to produce signals or convey ideas, it may be called a *figured* current. If we take a thick metal plate and make a red circle on one side, and a blue one the other, there will be a current through the plate from the red to the blue; but there will be no such current between the centers of the circles, except there should be an opposite one. This depends, however, on the size of the circles. We may paint any figures, and the sectional areas of the currents produced are like the figures. These currents are *sectionally figured*. To what distance a sectional figure can be preserved in a transelementary current, is difficult to say. It, evidently, depends on the electromotive force.

When a current is varied so as to represent sound waves, as in the telephone, or to be intermittent, magnetizing and demagnetizing a piece of soft iron for longer or shorter times, as in the telegraph, it may be said to be potentially varied.

PART IV.

ELECTRICITY IN ANIMAL ORGANISMS.

SECTION I.

THE GENERAL ELECTRIC STATE OF THE ANIMAL BODY.

It has been proven by experiments that electricity exists in the human body and, at the present time, there is, probably, no doubt on that point, though many believe that it is there accidentally and is not of any use. It is, however, difficult to say if it is fluid akasa or electricity.

In these days, when a closed electric circuit is largely used in art, the electricity in the organic kingdom is liable to be greatly misunderstood. Electricians expect to find electric circuits in animal organisms and in plants like those used in art. As a rule, there are no electric circuits in the organic kingdom. When a current runs over a nerve, it is positive and negative at different ends, or the current is an extension of an *inter-elementary* system, if it be not produced by a mystical psychic force. A tree is positive at the top and negative at the root, which acts in harmony with its *akasaic* system. It may be considered either as a thermic or photic generator, the top being green and exposed to heat, and the roots white, red, or orange and kept cool. The sap that rises in the plant, is elevated by both electric and akasaic force toward the top, where the electric current exhausts itself or is discharged into the air.

In some experiments on the resistance of the human body, the electric currents in the body have not been taken into account, and the results obtained have not been correct. It makes a great difference, whether the currents in the body are with or against that of the battery. If one of the hands are cold, a short wire, held over a slightly warm stove or in the flame of a candle, will produce a tinkling in the hand that is often greater than when a stronger battery is used.

In studying the electricity of animal bodies, we have first to deal with static electricity or, more exactly, with positive and negative electricity. The surface of the body is either positive or negative; it is neutral only when it passes from one electrification to the other. If there be a strong circulation of blood in the hands, they are very positive and will impart a slight charge to bodies with which they come in contact, which may be ascertained by any device used for studying static electricity. Exertion of any particular part makes that part negative. If a limb be very cold it is negative.

As a rule, the animal body is positive, because it is warm and has a negative structure, though some parts are more positive than others. The rule may be given that the body is most positive, where it has its greatest diameter. The chest of a man is more positive than that of a woman. When at rest, a healthy body has a positive spheroid around it whose diameter varies according to the state of the body and of the atmosphere. On the other hand, when the muscular tissue has been subject to general decomposition from activity or other causes, a negative spheroid is produced around the body.

Since the human body is either positive or negative, it has been thought that it should manifest attraction or repulsion in regard to other bodies. Especially has it been believed that his attraction is the cause of sexual affection. Electric repulsion and attraction, however, is of so little practical account that it can not be seen in very light bodies, except they are highly charged. The attraction between the different sexes, which many say exists in a material sense, is due, rather, to lines of akasa that instinctively stretch out from one person and takes another by the grip or surrounds him, as far as it can be understood. It is not due to electrification; for two bodies oppositely charged have rather a mutual repulsion, when they are a certain distance apart.

SECTION II.

VISIBLE EFFECTS OF THE FLOW OF ETHEREAL MATTER IN THE BODY.

The distribution of nourishment to the various parts of the organism is directly affected by the circulation of blood; the blood is forced around by the action of the heart; but whether the contraction of the heart is produced by intermittent electric currents, we can not say. There is a current over the nerves to a muscle when it contracts and it is probable that the contraction of muscles, generally, is helped by the action of electric currents or of fluid akasa. This we do not know; but it has been shown that an electric current will contract muscles after death.

There are currents, following the blood out through the arteries and inward through the veins; but whether they are causes or effects, can not be said. As they have a *carried* current outside of the surface of the body, they may be observed with a small astatic pendulum.

The distribution of the right kind of material to the various parts is, of course, affected by ethereal attraction, especially in the interior of bones; but all this can not be seen or studied directly.

It is a curious fact that, at those places on the surface of the human body where there are frequent discharges of ethereal matter, though not constantly, there are excrescences in the form of hair. As we can not distinguish between a flow of ethereal matter or fluid akasa and an electric current, we speak of the difference in the electromotive force of this discharge in different persons. Where this force is generally great, the hair is coarse and straight. As a highly positive condition of the half static electricity in the human organism, gives a current less force, those who have a more positive body have more curly hair, while the more negative have straighter. This same law applies to growths and formations in both the organic and the inorganic kingdom. Frost figures on windows are always curly and rich in appearance in a positive atmosphere, but straight and sharp in a negative one.

The direction in which hair lies also shows in which direction the discharged ethereal matter flows. The hair on the heads of humans has a vortex point a little behind the crown. This vortex is "with the sun" in the northern hemisphere; under the equator, there is no vortex; and, in the southern hemisphere, we should expect the vortex to be opposite to that in the northern, turning "with the sun" there, at least in aborigines. The division of hair at that point is due to a greater and more steady discharge at that place, and the vortex is due to the rotation of the discharged ethereal matter or electricity. Cattle and other animals have a vortex on the back directly over the stomach. The gyration of the charges in animal bodies are produced by friction against an east going current around the earth, as that of other charges.

The hairs on all animal bodies show in which direction electricity or surplus ethereal matter flows at every point, and also the comparative strength of the discharge. We may suppose, however, that gushes of akasa or akasaic organs produce some effect in this respect. If the hairs turn opposite to the natural direction in any place, this is a sign of an abnormal condition, but it seems most frequently to be produced by emanation of akasa.

When nutriment is deposited in the structure of the body, which must be affected by ethereal attraction or akasa or by both, ethereal binding material is needed. If we examine a region immediately around the surface of the body, we find an outward flow of either ethereal matter or akasa, that can be detected only to a distance of an inch or so from the surface, except that the hairs serve as a conduit for this flow. This ceases periodically and, during sleep or perfect rest, there is then a region around the surface of the body that presents all the characteristics of a "sphere of ethereal selection."* This occurs as regularly as in plants during perfect rest; but the regularity is disturbed by exertion, excitement, or other causes of decomposition of tissue. This selection only interrupts the positive spheroid around the body and, when there is a negative spheroid, the selection is irregular or can not be detected.

It is well known that muscular power is not always proportional to the size of the muscles. The strongest always discharge more electricity from their body and produce a greater sphere around them under similar circumstances.

That the electricity, in connection with the akasa, is not the product of power, but the cause, seems to be shown by the fact that neutralization of the electricity in the body, which disperses it, causes languor and weakness. Such neutralization takes place when bathing long in cold water or when a current from a battery is passed through the body. The power of certain organs are also lessened, when they receive a charge that is different from the natural one.

The muscles are, evidently, contracted by something similar to magnetic energy; for it may be observed that, during contraction, there is a current over the nerves to them and a circulation around them, as there is a very short current at right angles with it as long as it is contracted.

*See "Electricity as a Form of Ethereal Matter."

SECTION III.

SOURCES OF ELECTRICITY IN ANIMAL ORGANISMS.

The chief source of electricity in animal organisms is, of course, the food that is decomposed in the stomach. On the whole, food produces more negative than positive electricity, as it is of loose texture. There is, however, a great difference between different kinds of food in this respect. Hydro-carbonaceous food produces more positive electricity than nitrogenous, which is eminently negative.

The decomposing fluids in the body are chiefly saliva and pepsin. Like all corrosive and decomposing fluids, their own natural electrization is negative. Saliva seems to act on the hydro-carbonaceous parts of the food more readily than on the nitrogenous. However, it has a decomposing effect on all kinds of digestible food. For this reason, everything eaten should be well mixed with saliva.

Those foods that produce the most negative electricity are: animal tissue, such as lean meat; white of eggs; leguminous seeds, as beans and peas; fish; gluten in farinaceous substances; vegetables; cheese, in milk or separated; and acids and certain mineral salts. Those that are more positive are: sugars; starch; fat; salt; edible cartilage and bone; and yolk of eggs.

In the following table, the diameters of the natural surface charge and of the charge produced by the action of saliva are given for different substances, the bulk being about that of a grain of coffee in every case. The diameters, which are given in centimeters, are very great on account of the high temperature and the low electric capacity of the air at the time of the experiments.

Substances.	Surface Charge.	Charge by Saliva.
Sugar, loose.	40, positive.	494, positive.
Butter, salted.	44, "	84, "
Bread.	170, "	612, "
Yolk of eggs.	95, "	550, "
Tea, leaves.	52, "	110, "
Beef, raw.	216, "	642, negative.
White of eggs.	608, "	608, "
Grass, green.	26, "	190, "
Coffee roasted and whole 48, "		over 1000, positive.
Dry apples, sour.	38, negative.	78, negative.

Though the figures in the preceding list seem enormous, the electricity produced would, in no case, be perceptible. In hot weather, electricity spreads enormously, and a perceptible charge would spread through the air for many rods.

The action of saliva on some substances, as mustard, is peculiar. There seems to be a sudden obscure radiation in the opposite direction to that from which the saliva attacks it.

The chief production of electricity is in the stomach, where the food is more or less perfectly decomposed. As the ethereal matter in the structure of different substances seems to be proportional to their weight, we can best judge of the amount of electricity, that is produced by a certain amount of food, by noting what a mass of zinc of equal weight would yield.

To show the relative value of different foods as sources of energy, we give a table, showing the diameters of currents drawn by a dry bright zinc plate *over* a copper wire, about $\frac{3}{4}$ millimeter thick and 20 centimeters long, *from* each substance when moistened with pepsin. The zinc plate was 5 square centimeters and the substances were shaped into cubes so that a surface of 6 square centimeters were acted on by pepsin. The difference in the amount of electricity produced by the different substances is found by multiplying the sectional area of each current by its electromotive force.

the electromotive force is found approximately from the number of oscillations per minute of an astatic pendulum and is expressed in arbitrary units. The diameters are expressed in centimeters. To be exact we should make allowance for *carried* current and take only one third of the diameters given.

Substances.	Diameter of Currents.	E. M. Force.
Meat, lean roast.	13.	1.625
" " raw.	10.	1.1
" fat roast.	8.	1.17
Bread in pepsin and saliva.	8.4	1.54.
" in pepsin alone.	5.2	.87
" in saliva.	4.	.75
Raw fat	4.2	.613
Butter	6.4	1.115

The effect of the pepsin on the copper wire was simply to make its electrization like that of the dry zinc plate.

When an animal becomes weak on account of hunger, it is not because the tensile strength of the muscles has become less, but because there is very little ethereal energy. There is an increase of strength from the time mastication begins, long before the food is appreciably decomposed. However, we must keep in mind that weakness in animal organisms is not always a sign of the want of energy; it may be a sign that the energy is shut away for the time.

The animal body is, of course, not an insulator, and the electricity, produced during digestion, can escape quite easily. When the body is at perfect rest, such escape does not take place to a very great extent. This seems to indicate that it is converted into some ethereal forms of compounds and stored away for later use. This process may not be exactly like the charging of a storage battery; for the akasaic organism in the body controls the transformation of electricity to a greater or less extent. By the secondary or instinctive action of the soul, the physical laws, governing ethereal matter in the organism, are applied or suspended through the agency of the akasaic system. We may suppose the stomach to have an insulation of akasa. When exertion takes place after a meal, however, there is a great waste of electricity. Only a slight motion causes radiations of electric currents from the stomach. Beetles that are eager feeders have currents running out from their bodies, during meals, to a distance equal to 3 times the length of their bodies.

During digestion, the stomach and adjacent parts have, of course, the greatest charge. This charge rotates around an axis parallel to that of the earth, when it can. This is indicated by a vortex of hair on the back of animals that are steady feeders. As food yields more negative than positive electricity the first keeps the center, and the positive elements are, naturally, thrown to adjacent parts, to the heart and the lungs and to the abdomen. The increase in pulsation after a meal is probably caused by a greater positive state of the heart. The way the electricity flows from the stomach to the more positive parts, is shown by the direction of the hair on the sides.

The blood, naturally, takes up considerable of the positive element and carries it around in the body. Thereby, the extremities become positive, especially the upper, and the upper part at least, is in the same condition as an inter-elementary battery. Currents are chiefly along the spine upward and downward from the stomach, or forward and backward in quadrupeds. This may be observed with an astatic pendulum and is also indicated by the hair. The hair in the lower part of the neck of a person indicates upward currents, before they take on interior path inside the general flow that is eddying back over the skull.

There is a great waste of energy in animal organisms, especially in some of the lower. There is greater waste in quadrupeds than in a fish or a snake. Electric currents take a straight line, and the backward flow is, to a great extent, lost or keeps in growth an appendix, called the tail. In animals, in which electromotive force is small, as the elephant and the hog, there is less waste. This is also the case with those that occasionally walk on two legs, as the bear and the ape. The upward current, which is the greater, is, to a great extent, switched off on different nerves for use or transformed to be stored.

We see that the animal body is not a battery that is fitted to yield very much practical energy directly from the source. The electric energy has to pass through another process before it becomes available. The energy is made effective by the soul itself, which has mastery over the physical laws that govern electricity and ethereal matter. That it shall not be thought that we are only grasping after an explanation to help us out, we may keep in mind that a person's soul has such a control over ethereal matter outside of his body which has often been proven. With a torsion balance, for instance, a person can get any result he likes without touching it, if he does not expect a result too different from the true one. Neither need we worry about the lack of insulation around the body. The lines of akasa in the organism are the natural conductors of electricity in the nerves and outside of them, and they furnish also the insulation. After all, it seems unreasonable that the food should furnish all the energy that is used in an animal; but this is because we have no means of taking everything into account. As a transformer of electric energy, the animal organism is more perfect than any other machine. We may suppose that akasa furnishes part of the nerve power and that this source of energy is gathered from substances that we take no account of. Never, however, must we believe that electricity or a product similar to it is not the chief form of energy in the organism, whether it manifests itself through the nerves or through akasaic lines outside of the body.

Whatever we may think of the body as an electric battery, both electric elements are needed. The decomposed hydro-carbons produce material which is burned in the lungs where air is inhaled. This produces heat which again, produces positive electricity by heating the water in the body. Here, we have an important source of positive electricity beside that produced by digestion and thrown outside of the central charge of the stomach. By increasing the rate of respiration to the utmost, making it as deep as possible, we may in a minute produce such a positive state of the body that a slight anesthesia is experienced. This is due to a general neutralization of electricity throughout the whole body which gives no definite direction to currents, as the blood circulates all around and carries the heat or the positive charge with it. If rapid breathing has not this effect, the body has been highly negative, or the air has been so.

One of the causes of sleepiness is the want of positive electricity in the body; and that may be wanting even when the body is warm; for it is the heating of something, and not the heat, that that produces positive electricity. If we are required to be up at night, we can keep wide awake by eating sugar and drinking water, as sugar furnishes material for combustion in the lungs, and the water is heated.

Of course, light and heat from the outside, as well as atmospheric electricity, may furnish energy to the system or counteract the energy used in the body. A working man loses strength sooner in a negative atmosphere than in a positive. The influence of light may also be modified by the color of the skin; but this we can not discuss.

SECTION IV.

THE REGULATION OF ENERGY IN THE ORGANISM.

The ultimate control of all energy in animal bodies is exercised by that mysterious thing called consciousness. Physiology can not be well understood without taking consciousness and its manifestations, belief and will, into account. We may know that a current of electricity is running toward the brain; but on what nerves it will be switched off from there is a matter of uncertainty on account of the regulating consciousness. The seat of plain consciousness is considered to be at the base of the brain, or lower, where nerves from all parts of the body meet. There are, however, inferior seats of consciousness or of instinctive controling power both in the medulla oblongata and down through the spinal cord.

We can not understand how consciousness takes place, nor how that manifestation of it, called will, can regulate the practical actions of the body. Much less do we understand how there can be a secondary consciousness or instinct that knows what is to be done, and does it, when we are not even aware of the fact; but we must point out that such a regulating consciousness exists. It is this secondary consciousness that controls the energy sent over the nerves, as well as the separation and storing of energy. If this were superintended by our practical knowledge, we would fare very ill. When it is thought that all that takes place according to physical laws, we must say that secondary consciousness may prevent the action of such laws, if they do exist; hence it has the real control.

In the regulating action of both plain and secondary consciousness, there is made use of certain organs in the brain; but how they are set into activity is again a mystery. Some believe that the organs of will acts as a result of the effects of nervous currents, so that, if these currents could be traced and the system of conductors were known, we would know the resulting will. It seems, however, as if the relation of causes and effects is, is a great extent, nihilated at the point of consciousness. Not that a resolution or a will is without adequate causes; but these must be sought through the whole history of the subject as well as in the present.

The electric currents in the body do not run only through nerves. They run through veins and in other places. As they start from the battery, it may be put down as certain that the chief conductors are not nerves. For normal currents, lines of akasa seem always to be the natural conductors. These lines may run through nerves, or not. In order that electricity, when it is generated by digestion, shall not run at random through the body, we should expect an insulating sack of akasa around the stomach, which would also serve as the conduit in the right direction from there. It is after the electricity has reached the switches at the points in the conscious line from the brain down through the spine, that the nerves can be used as conductors, but the sensory nerves are never used as conductors for this electricity. The normal use of energy requires the motor nerves as conductors. There are also other applications of energy that are natural enough, though they may not be normal.

The regulating organs in the brain are situated under that part of the skull or scalp that is covered by hair. Those organs that are situated about the forehead and temples have an intellectual activity. When a person is, or is about to become, active, there is a discharge of current from the controlling organs. This may be observed by means of an astatic pendulum, when a person is lying down. If he moves any limb or muscle, there is one spot where the discharge ceases as long as the effort is kept up. Each limb or set of muscles has its particular spot where the discharge is stopped. As a rule, the position of the controlling organ is directly opposite to the position or the limb or muscle controled. The crown corresponds to the feet; the lower part of the back head, to the forehead; and the sides of the head, to the sides of the body.

Secondary consciousness has other actions than that of regulating utilized energy. An example of this may be had, when a person goes to sleep with the fixed determination to wake at a certain hour. During the sleep, there must then be a keeping of time in some way; for a person generally wakes on the very minute he intended to do so.

Secondary consciousness also counteracts disagreeable currents of negative electricity, that run in through the body from the atmosphere as the effects of drafts, by sending currents against them or in other ways. This is kept up until the nuisance ceases or until the regulating consciousness yields. If this process of resisting and yielding takes place on two or more successive days, the time-keeping tendency of consciousness makes it a habit. The feeling of resistance and final breaking down occurs regularly at the same time of day that it happened before, without any outward reality as cause. It is, evidently, in this way intermittent fevers arise.

SECTION V.

THE SENSES.

Sense impressions are transmitted to the seat of consciousness by inward currents over the sensory nerves. We have intimated that some sensations are not transmitted to plain consciousness at once. We can not explain how consciousness takes note of the sense impressions; but an inward current on the visual nerves often produces the sensation of a spot of light and intermittent currents from the ear produce the sensation of a sound.

The brain has also a certain control over the organs of sense. During rest they are all positive under normal circumstances which prevents the transmission of sensations. When they are to be used, the body is given a more or less wide negative margin where the organs are situated. Those persons that are least positive and can receive the greatest negative margin, are the most sensitive.

Sight.—Sight and hearing are the most interesting of all the sensations, because they can be most easily understood from physical laws, excepting the consciousness of the sensations. The eye contains a transparent fluid, protected by a tough transparent covering without. Behind this is an adjustable opening, the pupil, and a concave lens. This part of the eye is the focusing apparatus and is equal to a convex and a concave lens. In the inner part of the eye, at the termination of the visual nerves, is a black mass, called the retina, which receives the rays admitted. The light admitted to the retina is, naturally, converted into electricity and ethereal compounds, corresponding to the amount and character of the light at different points in the lighted spot.

We can not say with certainty whether the light itself produces an inward current, or not. This is greatly helped, if not entirely produced, by regulation in the organism in the case of blue light. The electric state of the eye, when it is active, may be ascertained by means of an astatic pendulum and a comparing or testing apparatus, consisting of a metal ball at one end of a wire and a metal ring to be laid over the eyelids at the other.

The representation of that which is seen is, without doubt, transmitted over the visual nerves by means of what we have called figured currents. The figure in the sectional area, we may suppose to consist of different ethereal compounds, produced in the retina.

Ocular spectra afford admirable means of studying the behavior of the representations that are presented to the point of consciousness of vision, when they are overdone by being prolonged beyond the natural time or made more than naturally strong. Ocular spectra are bright changing visions of an object after it has been stared at for some time against a very strong light. The effect of keeping a current, conveying a very strong image, for a long time is to make the image unfit to be recorded in the organs of memory. It is then managed in some other way; for a mental image has a reality just as much as a painting or a statue. After looking at a bright object and then shutting the eyes, the image disappears; but soon an image springs up which changes in different colors; disappearing now and then. We always find that an ocular spectrum, as soon as it emerges from the dark, is blue.

Hearing is easily understood from the transmission of sound by wave motion of electricity or intermittent currents. The other senses are more mysterious. The scenting of dogs and other animals has been considered the same as smell; but it is difficult to believe that it is.

SECTION VI.

THE INTELLECTUAL ORGANS.

The intellectual organs of the brain are situated about the forehead and temples, or below that part of the skull that is not covered by hair. Some of these have always been considered as organs of memory. That memory requires organs is quite certain, and there must also be apparatus or receptacles where sense impressions are recorded. We advanced the theory that ocular spectra were caused by the bulkiness of the image, whereby they become too coarse to be recorded in the delicate and minute receptacles used for that purpose. Anatomy will not reveal any direct signs of such recorded representations, and we have to note carefully all outward manifestations.

When the eye observes an object, there is an outward current to some of the organs in the center of the forehead or in the lower part, according to what is observed about the object. These currents are discharged into the air and may be easily observed.

We have no reasons for not taking the names, used by phrenologists, to designate the different parts of the forehead, instead of the divisions of anatomists. We will subdivide them into three classes: organs of simple record in the lower part of the forehead; organs of comparison in the upper part; and organs of harmony about the temples.

The phrenological names of the organs of simple record are: eventuality, individuality, form, size, weight, color, order, number, locality, and time, and, besides them, tune and language that are organs for the recording of sound. Number and order also belong to the group of organs that record harmony; for there is a gradual transition from one class to another. The organs for comparison are: comparison (of particulars); causality; mirth; imitation; agreeableness; and intuitive knowledge of human nature. The uppermost of these are also organs of feeling. The organs of harmony are: tune, constructiveness, imitation, ideality, and some others. All these organs are controled by the controlling organs just above the cerebellum.

Experiments show that there are also outward currents to an organ, when anything is called up from memory. An excellent device for studying this is the "phrenological cap." This may consist of common cloth and fit quite closely. It is pierced by pins or rivets whose heads press against the organ. To the other end of the rivets are fastened short wires of good cenductivity that may terminate in a strip of wood, placed horizontally. When an organ is active, there is a current over the wire that is discharged at the other end, where it may be observed. It runs so slowly, however, that it may be doubted whether it is common electricity, and the effect of the activity of the organ comes afterward.

It has been noticed that, when a person tries to remember how an object moved, or how it changed, the organ of eventuality is active. It is also active when we imagine motion or change. Imagination puts also the organs into activity, and so does thinking.

When we make use of memory, we call up the very same images that were once brought before the point of plain consciousness from without. They are only diminished and faded and are, probably, brought up again before a weaker point in the conscious line. If we dwell on memory in imagination the images again become as bright as before. It is thought that imagination can make original images quite easily; but it is not easily done if they are wanted very plain; but such plain imagination is also a nuisance and should never be indulged in.

Thinking is, evidently, a more or less complicated sending of ideal representations back and forth between the intellectual organs and the consciousness of thought. The memory of feelings or, to speak more exactly, the receptacles for representations of them seem to be in other parts of the organism than the brain, and their transmission to consciousness is often considerably retarded.

Thinking consumes just as much electric energy as bodily exertion. It will be observed that if a person carries a heavy weight, he is tempted to drop it, if he is asked a question that he does not even intend to answer. Electric energy is needed in intellectual work and, if it is not readily furnished by digestion, the tissues of the body is consumed to furnish it.

There is a theory, originated in the Gatta of Goths that thinking makes use of thought signs, and not images. These are, of course, smaller than many of the recorded images and require very little printer's ink, so to speak; but the material has to be furnished and applied, nevertheless. In making mental imagery, however, it is quite certain, according to testimony, that the weak and emaciated make them more faded than those that are healthy. Here, we must not confound mental imagery with hallucinations, which are believed to be transferred from others and then taken up before the point of plain consciousness.

SECTION VII.

DIGESTION AND REPAIR OF THE ORGANISM.

Since nerve energy is of so great an importance, it is also important to know how it is best furnished. Supply of nerve energy and repair of the tissues go together, so we must also mention what kind of food is most needed for the repair of the body. Much may have been written on food and digestion; but the difficulty is that those who best understood the art of digestion never write much on any subject, and those who study and write much seldom know the art of digestion

In the selection of food, the main point is to get what is needed to build up the tissues, namely hydro-carbons for combustion in the lungs, and nitrogenous matter for the repair of the tissue. Hydro-carbonaceous matter is nearly always present in sufficient amount, while the nitrogenous part is insufficient.

"Examining different kinds of nitrogenous food, we find animal flesh in a fresh state at the head of the list. It contains exactly the same elements as the tissues of the body. The juices contain the mineral salts and, if these are extracted by salt, the flesh is less valuable. Next in the list we may place eggs; the albumen is nitrogenous and the yolk contains fat and mineral salts. Milk, when new, ranks very high, the curd or casein is nitrogenous, and the cream contains fat. Cheese is not as valuable as might be supposed, and gluten in bread is less easily assimilated than flesh."

"A meal, taken without disagreeable disturbance of any kind, should always produce a calm, content, and good natured feeling. If it does not, the digestion is poor, or the selection of food is not well made; for digestion will, generally, be best when nitrogenous and carbonaceous foods are present in the right proportion. Poor digestion produces discontent and a dead feeling about the stomach. This is always felt when a poor selection is made. If meat alone be eaten, a person will gather considerable strength from it; but there is a feeling of discontent. The same is the case if bread alone be eaten, though in a less degree. A mixture of food always produces the best results, and the mixture should also be regulated by feeling; for that is a better guide than any prescribed rules."

"A meal should be eaten slowly, and, as digestion sets in, a stimulus is felt. It is from this time on, that we may have occasion to practice the art of digestion under the guidance of this pleasurable feeling. If the least morsel of any food seems to lower the state of your feeling, do not take another of the same kind until you feel different; for a single morsel will sometimes neutralize the stimulus instantly, except in those whose digestion is insured against anything. Take another kind of food, until you think you feel a slight attack of dullness. You may eat of the former kind of food again. In many places in Europe, it is customary to regulate digestion by keeping a cup of coffee by their side and sipping it for an hour or so after a meal. It is by such careful observation of the dictates of feelings, that a person with a naturally poor digestion can learn to digest his food." Anatol Trolladeen.

It is during sleep, that the tissues are most perfectly repaired. There is, then, a general flow of currents outward to the surface of the body, interrupted at regular intervals, which indicates that matter is deposited. The currents from the head, however, are less easily observed. The repair, without doubt, goes on all the time, where a person does not work with such continuous effort that he does not rest a minute or so now and then.

SECTION VIII.

THE EFFECT OF DIFFERENT ELECTRIC AND ETHEREAL CONDITIONS ON HEALTH

The natural electrization of an animal body is positive at the surface. Negative electricity from without always produces a bad effect. A slight chill is felt more in a negative atmosphere than a much lower temperature in a positive one. Negative electricity in the animal organism should always start from the stomach. On account of the greater fluency of negative electricity, it also penetrates the body very easily.

Natural sources of negative electricity are drafts of cold air, especially those that come through small apertures, as they are negative in opposition to the warmer air; fog and condensation of vapors; a horizontal position of the moon in a moist atmosphere; and decomposition of negative metals.

The feeling produced by sultry weather is that of negative electricity in a warm state of the air. In negative fog, the feeling of shivering and chill is replaced by that felt in sultry weather, as soon as the sun is high enough to warm it. It has been noticed that rheumatism and neuralgia is not produced by cold and damp where the air is positive. Positive electricity has always a soothing influence.

To find out what effect negative electricity has on the organism, one may decompose zinc in sulphuric acid; but, as it spreads through the air very easily, it ought to be entirely enclosed or insulated, with the exception of the conductor. We would not advise any one to try this more than once, however, except he has a very positive body that will neutralize it. The effect, when zinc is rapidly decomposed, is first to produce a mild tinkling through the arms and then a disagreeable pressure in the region of the heart. Soon, cramp in the fingers may also begin. If the experiment be repeated often, a person will acquire a habit of shivering and also a pressure at the heart.

Those who handle type metal a good deal, as in printing offices, experience effects of this kind. Their antidote is alcohol. Under the action of decomposing fluids, this is highly negative.

PART V.

AKASA AND AKASAIC ORGANISMS.

SECTION I.

IDEAS OF AKASA AND THE SOUL.

Akasa is, generally, considered a part of the soul or that form of matter of which the soul consists. In a scientific treatise on this form of matter, we can not say that it is the soul or a part of the soul; for the idea soul has never been defined from a material point of view. We have a vague idea that the soul is the ultimate life principle of animal organisms; but those who have defined the idea or written the most about the soul deny that it is material. If it is not matter of some kind; it must be only a condition of matter, for nothing exists that is not matter or a condition of matter. Those who have written on the soul, however, seem to be unwilling to admit that it is either, though they say it is something. This want of logic and philosophical exactness need not bother us much. We only point it out. We say that, if the soul exist, it is matter and, presumptively, imponderable matter, or it is a condition of matter.

Nearly all of the most eager students of psychology show very little interest in physical researches on the imponderable and more subtle forms of matter and ignore some of the more well known physical laws. Psychologists of the liberal kind have many theories that are only absurd, because they are at variance with well known physical laws. It has been said that a person can go into a trance and send his soul to distant places, while it is connected to the body only by means of "a string of electricity." What it is palpably false here is that it is connected to the body in that way; for electricity is not strung out for any length of time, except on a surface where the electrification were produced in that way. However, we can not say that there is not a current of electricity between the main part of the soul and the body, if the soul can leave it in that way, which we do not know. What we must say is that electricity needs a conductor, and we do not see how those easy talkers can find a suitable conductor for an electric current through the air, directed, not at random, but so exactly that it serves as the connection between the soul on its roving trip and the motionless body.

We mention all this, only because the ideas of the most advanced psychologists are mixed up with false theories like this. By "most advanced psychologists" we mean those who are not fettered by prejudice and take note of all abnormal psychic phenomena and combine their study with experiments or practice in order to find how they take place step by step.

In the Gatta of the Goths, a course of psychical research, the idea prevailed that no psychical phenomenon can take place contrary to the laws of matter. According to that idea the soul of one person can not see through the body of another; an opaque body can not be transparent. The soul of one person may gradually learn to know the condition of the body of another; and the result may be presented to consciousness in the form of a picture of a transparent body. It is also doubtful if a person's soul leaves the body and soars over the ground. To a person's consciousness it may appear so, especially since a new scene appears before our inner eye every time we make a halt. But this feeling of roaming around is only a faculty of amusing himself which every person possesses to a greater or less degree. One thing is very certain; a person's soul, if the akasaic organs be the soul, can not penetrate solid, coherent matter as a thick, tight wall; for it finds difficulty in penetrating, partially, the clothing on the body, even when this is thin. The laws of matter are the fundamental laws of the soul.

The dark-skinned races are those who formerly have been best acquainted with the secrets of the soul. These people believe in the life of the soul after it has left the body; but the most of them do not like to bury the body undecomposed, at least not in a tight or tightly walled grave. The American Indians leave the body on a high scaffolding, until it is decayed. The Indians proper or the Hindus burn the body. It is the belief of some that the soul is so knitted together with the organs of the body that it takes time before the soul can completely leave it.

Among all these conflicting ideas of the soul, it is a little too bold to give detailed accounts of experiments that are new and say that we have experimented on the human soul or the matter of which the soul is made. Almost everybody would be against that. The most numerous writers say the soul is not material, and the most exact investigators say that there is no soul. The best way is to tell systematically what we have found, and let people call it something closely connected with the soul or a peculiar force acting outside of the nerves. Many who have been eager to find some signs of the existence of the soul or of something that might be looked on as akin to the soul, must get rid of the idea, that a thorough knowledge of the movements of ethereal matter is useless here. It is by means of a thorough knowledge of such currents that we can distinguish between ether and akasa.

SECTION II.

EXPERIMENTS ON AKASA AND ETHEREAL CLOUDS.

When we undertake various experiments on currents or movements of ethereal matter in the atmosphere, we notice something that will be considered either as "nothing" or as ethereal matter of a non-fluid consistency. There are spots where an astatic pendulum will not only not have any definite direction of motion for want of any current to act upon it; but it is held still by a certain force, which must be due to something. We have called these phenomena ethereal clouds and ethereal compounds of a non-fluid consistency. If we are wrong, we do not like to have any one tell us so; for those who would contradict this, would naturally be somethat knew nothing about it. Now, these ethereal clouds can be neutralized by other ethereal clouds or by friction of something and by heat and light. This seems to prove that the blank spots in the atmosphere are something.

This something may be quite general throughout the atmosphere at times, as in cold and sultry weather. Currents of this matter are never found, except when there are general electric currents through the atmosphere in a certain direction. Then the supposed non-fluid matter is set adrift, and is noticeable by its violent action on the pendulum that indicates it.

Where this non-fluid matter occupies a small space, an electric or ethereal current passes through it and may be detected on both sides of it. Spheres of such matter are always formed around an object that is solidifying or is taking up matter infused into it as in growth, &c. It has been often said that everything has a soul from the broken fragment of a stone to the crystal; but these coarse spheres can not be the souls of these objects for they disappear, when the object is not in a process of growing or solidifying, except they should sink together into the interior of the objects to which they belong. However, all objects have a considerable sphere around them, throughout which they have a varied influence. These spheres can not be detected by anything but their effects, and we would be more inclined to call them the souls of the inanimate bodies. That the coarser spheres sink into the interior of matter when this is in a normal and finished condition seems to be beyond doubt. It may be called out again, though irregularly, by rubbing. This process produces electricity and a streak of a coarser material phenomenon that wavers back and forth and is not yet distinguished from the akasa produced by an animal body. There is, in the language of the Gattaists, an *al-ak te re*.

If we stroke a surface with the hand back and forth once, there is left a streak of akasa that oscillates back and forth the same way it was stroked. If the stroking was entirely or principally in one direction, the line of akasa keeps moving or running in that direction. If there are currents of electricity or ether in the atmosphere, the akasaic line will drift slowly along with them and can be detected in the air at different points of its course. However, it reappers on the stroked surface now and then, rising up from the interior of the substance, but only to drift away again. If a friction of metal takes place near a stroked line, the line of akasa is disturbed or forced out of place, at least at the point nearest to the disturbance. If volatile substances be brought near, or even oil when agitated or rubbed, they will have the same effect.

When there is no disturbance of any kind around, and the air is clear, mild, and calm, a long strip of wood, free from metal and oil spots, may be stroked, a person may touch different points on that line, and those points can be detected by means of an astatic pendulum. If the akasaic line is touched in one place only, there is no difficulty in finding it, as an astatic pendulum oscillates back and forth over the line, but suddenly hangs still when brought over the touched point. As the akasaic lines are sometimes "dead" and sometimes oscillating, the pendulum will begin to oscillate over the touched point, if it were hanging still before. The touching of such lines of akasa brings to light many curiosities which we cannot mention here.

"In a place where several people frequently gather, as in a school house, there may be a considerable charge of akasa extending outside of the house. Such charges have radiations from it extending in all directions with uniform distances between each arm. When not disturbed, these arms are quite durable. It is a laborious task, however, to find them. It may be remarked that persons of quiet phlegmatic habits have such charges of akasa around their abodes. Such a system of akasaic lines seems to have been called *fram* or *bram lines* in the Gatta of Goths. Others, however, insist that the right name is *am* and that *fram* is a strong line in one direction. Anatol Trolladeen.

SECTION III.

THE TENDENCY OF AKASA TO BECOME ORGANIC.

We notice that charges of akasa stretch out arms in all directions which have considerable permanence. If such a charge be developed around the dwelling place of a person it remains after he leaves the place. If the akasaic organism in a person's body be the soul, this charge is a soul without a body, a soul that has reached *nirvana*. The akasaic organism in the body of a person is a system stretching out arms in all directions from the spinal column; and secondary radiations of smaller extent from the various nerve centers that are more or less controlable by a person's will.

"We can not look on such developments (charges of akasa) simply as a growth but as an organ used for some purpose, the means of transmitting ideas from soul to soul. Plegmatic persons who take everything so cool, are always on the safe side; for they act as if they did know the facts in every case all around, even if it is not in their primary consciousness. It is around them the fram lines are developed so that they can not be detected. In other cases they can not be detected, though they, no doubt, exist, as surely as we expect to find them in the sphere of influence of an inanimate body." Anatol Trolladeen.

Akasa may be found everywhere throughout space; but we know nothing about it. It is quite certain that we find it developed in greatest abundance where there is considerable moisture. We have heard that when two snails are kept near together for some time and then taken a distance apart, they will both act alike, move in the same directions, &c. We do not know if this is so; but the story shows that people have noticed something about moist animals before, and probably, wanted to transmit their knowledge to posterity in a set story. It is also interesting to read the account of the liberated souls or spirits who move through dry places and then try to take possession of a person's body, making a maniac of the same according to old ideas. We may also note a very wide-spread idea that it is well for maniacs to take baths very often.

Anatol Trolladeen in his novel "From India to Mars" makes a Buddhist priest say: "Do you know that a line of akasa has the faculty of locomotion?" Those who experiment on akasa and study psychology by taking it into account get that impression; but it is difficult to prove it.

When the *amoeba princeps*, a jelly-like lump developed in water, is believed to have a spontaneously generated life, this is concurred in quite readily by those who have studied akasa; for akasa develops an apparent life, and there is no life without an akasaic system of organs, and some of these seem to act so independently of the main consciousness at times, that a person, for instance, appears to be a complete double-being, both parts endowed with reason.

SECTION IV.

GUSHES OF AKASA FROM ANIMAL ORGANISMS.

It is said by some that they can feel, at times, a peculiar stirring sensation when a person in the vicinity is angry, even when they do not see him, or he makes no demonstration. It is not easy to make some people believe that something that they can not see or feel does exist. As a general thing we can not see or feel akasa; but movements of it may be detected by an astatic pendulum.

If a person stands on one side of a room and has his whole attention turned to some point on the opposite wall, there will be a strong current from his face to that point which will last for a short time and will be indicated by an astatic pendulum placed in its path. When the current ceases, there is a dead quiet in the line of the current; but on all sides there is a backward flow of the same depth as the diameter of the central current. If the person takes his attention away from that point or thinks of it no longer with any interest, the backward flow on the outside ceases, and the central current flows back; that is, it seems to sink back into the body. This movement of akasa can be detected in all conditions of the atmosphere, where no other experiments with pendulums are possible. When electric currents in the atmosphere are general and very strong, the movement of akasa may be disturbed at certain moments; but, as a general thing, the movement of akasa does not yield.

Where this phenomenon is known, the young people detect such movements of akasa by holding a pendulum in the hand quite carelessly, while the person who is to force a line of akasa to a distance is placed behind a veil so his face can not be seen, as the direction might be guessed from its expression. He is generally given three or four points to choose between, and search is made only in those lines; for rapidity is necessary.

as the person behind the veil may have to strain his mesmeric faculties. These experiments have not yet been known to fail.

It is not possible to force akasa through a tight cloth or a sheet of metal. Movements of akasa are always noticed, when a person is interested in an object near, or when he mesmerizes another.

The akasa that proceeds from the body very often goes to a certain point where it terminates in a dead quiet where pendulum experiments are impossible. Many who try such experiments make them impossible by their own interest or anxiety. If several interested persons came together to witness such pendulum experiments they are simply made impossible. They have to be looked at carelessly or looked at as little as possible. We have to say this here; for it is seldom we can say it. We have to shake our head and point to the sky. It must not be believed that sight does it; it is the interest that is felt. We must not listen to it with interest; for that would have the same effect.

All the different radiations of akasa from the body, are not controled alike by will. Some are probably not controled by conscious will. This seems to be the case with the lines that extend directly from the spine or neck as well as from the throat and upper forehead. It appears also in some places where akasa is forced out by long continued willing, it finally obeys, but is out for a long time contrary to will.

The use of the regular lines of akasa from the body is, without doubt, the transference of ideas from both secondary and primary consciousness to the minds of others. As organs of the mind we must consider the conscious line through the spinal cord with its arms of akasa. There are different degrees of clear consciousness from the base of the brain downward. Ideas transferred to certain points of consciousness are hardly known; but they are acted out. This is found by experiment; for many mesmerists do not affect others by a blind force of their mind, but by transferring to them a list of instructions that are acted sure enough and are not known otherwise. This is what was called witchcraft formerly and does not so act immediately as common mesmerism, neither does it bring a person into an abnormal position.

While transference of ideas is the most common use of the arms of akasa, they are also used for direct and original observation of some kind. We do not know if we can call it sight; it may be. Clairvoyance, in the sense that a person's soul can see through anything, opaque bodies or transparent ones. never exists. What is called clairvoyance is the gathering of transferred knowledge and knowledge due to second sight in regard to something. One can never see through a person's body as some impostors make believe. Second sight is a laborious examination of an object by piecemeal and never figures greatly in the remarkable feats of the soul. Clairaudience is a reproduction in sound signs of transferred ideas. One can never hear, what can not be heard by the ear. The fancied sound is an hallucination invented by the soul and may be more important than if it were a *fac-simile* of some talk.

Some people feel the presence of certain metals intuitively; others do not feel them, but will find them easily by means of a twig, &c. All this is due to second feeling or sight.

With the idea that thoughts are transferred from one to another without their knowledge, and that they are acted out blindly, we see no difficulty in defending the theory of predestination and fate in the chief events of history. The minor events are predestined at least a minute before they occur; but some are destined to take place months, and others years, before the time of occurrence has come.

SECTION V.

THE ACTION OF AKASAIC LINES OUTSIDE OF THE ORGANISM.

We have mentioned before that the lines of akasa have an effect on ethereal matter outside of the body. This effect consists in the production of movements, either currents or to and fro movements of ethereal matter or akasa. There may also be produced a condition similar to "ethereal clouds." All this can be produced at will, but these conditions are also produced by a person without his will and knowledge.

On a table, the currents of electricity in the atmosphere may be examined by some person. If you *will* and imagine that there are currents over the table from north to south, the experimenter will find it that way even with the most perfect instrument. If you will that the "currents" change, the instrument indicates the change. These currents, or oscillations which they really are, are produced at the end of a line of akasa from the person who has his mind directed to a certain point. At the termination of the line of akasa, there may be produced vortices, "dead spaces," and "currents." The reader will readily understand that it is possible for a person to falsify the indication of an astatic pendulum instrument any time without being detected. An astatic pendulum is not reliable, except people are away from it and its indications are registered.

Great mistakes have been made by some on this account. Foucault found that a swinging pendulum with a fixed support turned or changed oscillation from north and south to west and east in 6 hours near the north pole, or turned around completely in 24 hours, while in South America it lost time in some way, it is immaterial which way; for the experimenter got results as he needed them, as he was always near anxiously watching his pendulum.

As the soul has a secondary consciousness, holding facts

gathered by the akasaic organs of the body, we are not led astray very much by the false currents produced by the fancy of a person. Where there is no determined will to deceive, these currents represent a fact in nature, known only to the soul. The currents themselves, however, may be false, or they may be greatly fortified, while the natural ones can not be noticed.

Many pendulum experiments are of the same kind as that of Foucault. There is truth below somewhere, but not always in the experiment itself. We do not know what to say about the detection of the age of an organic substance. If a cube of wood be examined, it is found to have a sphere around it in which there are currents to or from the wood. If we touch the cube of wood lightly with a small stick, the sphere is found to shrink for every stroke or touch. It has sunk entirely into the wood, when the wood has been touched as many times as the age of the wood has years. This is true in a clear, mild and calm atmosphere. In some conditions of the atmosphere it has to be touched more times, and sometimes the sphere disappears with fewer touches. There may be some connection between the age of, and the sphere around, a substance; but the phenomenon may also be produced by the akasaic organs of the experimenter whose soul has perceived in the structure of the substance its real age.

Communication with the surrounding world is so necessary for the well-being of mankind that it takes place through considerable distances, as is brought to light by certain experiments. The communication, in this case, is not of a lengthy kind, but short and often repeated, as we may suppose. In this case, we suppose that the communication takes place by means of vibrations through the cosmic ether. There is no special line of communication, but the message is sent in the right direction and repeated. Instinct dictates the vibrations to be sent, and it is brought to secondary consciousness only in a general way. When a person is in distress, another person may get a vague idea about it at the same time at quite a distance. Fear is always necessary to produce such signals. Under other circumstances, each person is supposed to transmit his fundamental ideas around indefinitely, and many feel condemned if their ideas are different from those around, even if they have heard nothing about them. The Gattaists call this *oming*, while the sending of a message in one direction is called *anning*.

"Conservative people are generally *om* people. They are generally short, thick and solid-built. These people can not hold a new idea alone. They feel condemned and despised. To make a proselyte of such a person, it is not necessary to talk much; but go around in his neighborhood and imagine how you would talk to him, and how he would acquiesce. You must do this all around him, though not in every house; but you must imagine that his worst enemies are against." Anatol Trolladeen.

The Gattaists also speak of *ang*, an echo in one place of ideas in another. According to them, Christianity furnishes means of maintaining *aug* between Europe and Africa, besides being the staff on which the christian leans through the valley of the shadow of death. "He had to be put to death for our sake" is the idea in Europe. "He has to be killed for the safety of others" say the Africans, and they kill a man or woman every day. The Gattaists believe that the wholesale killing would not go on, if it were not for the *ang* with Europe which makes them feel as if it were necessary and quite innocent.

The Gattaists call the distance that oming has any visible effect the *rak* or *rok*. Senlac in South Brittain, according to them, was the rak (reach) of oming from the Seine. It should be Senrak. Thick *l*, like thick *r*, was used in North Gaul and South Brittain.

SECTION VI.

THE CONTROLING ORGANS OF THE BRAIN AND SUPPOSED ORGANS OF RECORD.

We have said that consciousness controls the action of the nerves by means of organs. The seat of the organs are, in the human species, covered by hair. During activity there is a constant escape of electricity through the hairs of the head; but from the special controlling organ that does service at any time, the flow is stopped. It is readily supposed that the controlling organ turns part of the current from the stomach back over the nerves; but how it is done we can not say.

If we stretch a band 2 or 3 inches wide over the head from the neck to the forehead, we cover a set of organs that control the anterior and posterior part of the body all around. The lower part of the back of the head controls the upper part of the forehead. Those groups that are higher control respectively the different parts of the face. Those still higher control the front of the body. The highest part in front of the vortex controls the feet, &c. The organs on the sides of the head are in connection with the opposite sides of the body.

It is well known that different groups of these organs are named by phrenologists as the organs of certain moral faculties or certain instincts. It seems to be entirely wrong to speak about organs of feelings, as pity. An *organ* is an instrument for *working*. "Organ" and "working" have the same origin. It is quite sure, however, that a great development of the different controlling organs indicate a corresponding development in certain feelings and propensities. What the phrenologists call "firmness" controls the feet and legs. It is natural that one who can stand firmly on his feet, is firm in other things.

As there are two kinds of consciousness, a primary and a

secondary, so there are recording organs for both kinds; at least our reason expects that there should be. Some psychologists hold that there are recording organs all through the body, which record facts in regard to the secondary action of the soul and also serve as organs for the preservation of prenatal knowledge.

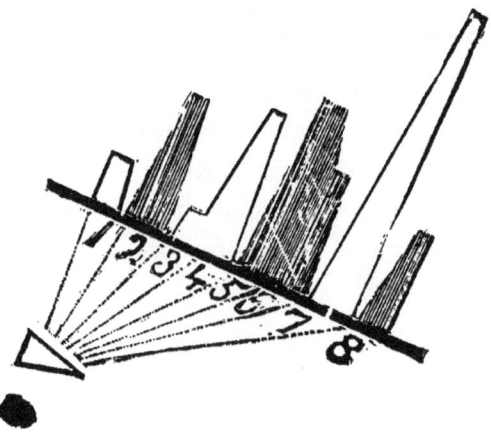

Representation of the invisible spectrum, showing the extent to which the air is electrified opposite each of the elements; the streaked regions are negative; the blank, positive.

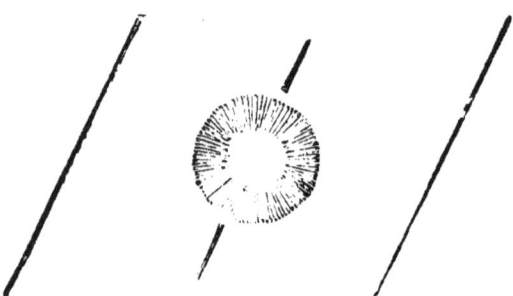

Representation of a positive electrosphere, showing the periphery of its cylinder and the axis of rotation.

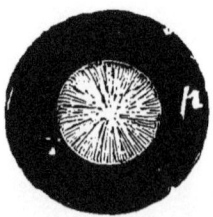

A negative electrosphere without its cylinder.

The following works are now ready for the press:

REPORT OF THE GATTA OF THE GOTHS
By Anatol Trolladeen. Illustrated.

This work is simply unique. It is the result of a research of an uncommon kind. The work contains nothing but notes written in a hypnotic or a half-hypnotic state by a party of men interested in psychology and history, except that the author has furnished the connecting links between the different notes or has given the general gist of them only where they have been too faulty in grammatical respects. This is a treatise on the secrets of psychology, and yet all throught it treats of history or, rather, of prehistoric times. The notes all through the book uphold the theory that a person has a knowledge of prenatal events which is only in his secondary consciousness, and that intinct in animals is such an inborn or prenatal knowledge. The work shows that humanity has a mental language of which they have only a secondary consciouness. This is evidently the foreign tongues spoken of by Paul. Some notes are too "transcendent" for some readers; but they have made themselves, so to speak, and nobody is to blame.

It is with exceeding pleasure that we read of the speculations in prehistoric times, be it truth or fiction. Yet the assertions in this work are bold, and there are ideas that have scarcely entered the minds of men before. For this reason, the author and his companions did not have the courage to publish this work or to be known as the authors of it. It is at considerable expense that N. Kolkin has made it his property.

FROM INDIA TO MARS
By Anatol Trolladeen. Illustrated.

This is a novel in the Jules Verne style. In this novel a Frenchmen is made the inventor of the astatic pendulum electroscope, and one of the characters in the novel makes practical use of this, thereby accomplishing what would otherwise be impossibilities.

Look out for these Books and ask your bookseller for them.

ELECTRICITY
AS A FORM OF ETHEREAL MATTER
—— BY ——
N. KOLKIN.

This work, of which "Ethereal Matter, Electricity, and Akasa" is an extract, was advertised and was intend to be published as early as 1887 by Farnes & Rothie, of Minneapolis. As Mr. Farnes suddenly died and there was no written agreement with the firm, nothing more than the advertising was done. Generally, the different theories in this work are based chiefly on experiments with astatic pendulums which have been carried on by the author for several years. The results of the experiments have been communicated to the International Society of Electricious at Paris (see the bulletin of the society for 1885), and some of the experiments were explained in papers presented to the Minnesota Academy of Natural Sciences at Minneapolis in 1886. Mr. Kolkin is also the real inventor of the astatic pendulum electroscope, though the peculiarities of such pendulums have been discovered by many others.

The work contains several chapters on each of the following subjects: Conservation of energy, fixed electric currents and charges, the laws of fluids, magnetism, astronomy, and ethereal currents in vegetables. All subjects are treated of more fully than in the extract made from it.

The delay in publishing this work is due to the important fact that several parts of it are based on experiments, the correctness of which it is desirable to prove beyond the possiblity of cavil beforehand.

The work will contain numerous illustrations and consist of about 300 pages. It will be published as soon as possible.

www.ingramcontent.com/pod-product-compliance
Lightning Source LLC
Chambersburg PA
CBHW022143090426
42742CB00010B/1362